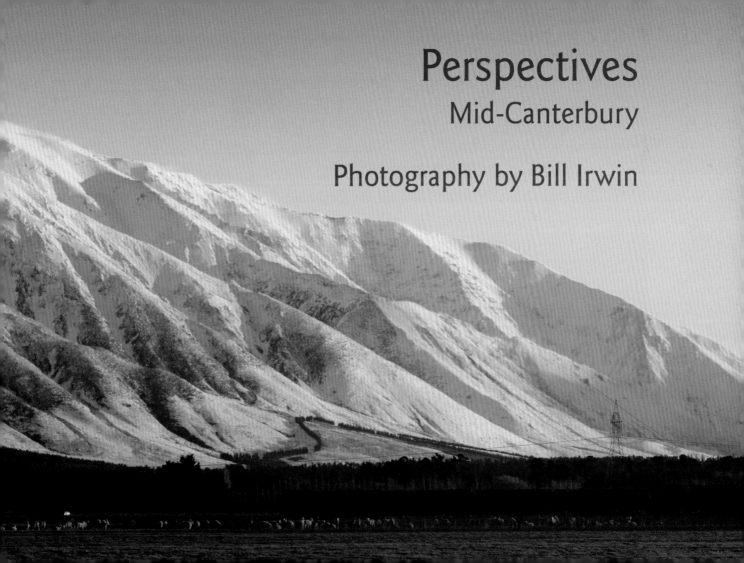

Perspectives
Mid-Canterbury

Photography by Bill Irwin

Tussock, Maori Lakes

Front cover: Cattlestop,
Erewhon Road
Back cover: View over the
Canterbury plains
Previous pages:
Page 1: Plains and mountains
from a balloon
Pages 2 & 3: Dawn light
on Mt Hutt

Opposite: Water bubbles up
through a sheet of thin ice on
a frosty morning at Lake Camp

Tussock on Mt Hutt, high above the Rakaia River and Canterbury plains

Opposite: Potts River, from the road to Erewhon

Mailbox near the turn-off to Mt Possession Station

Opposite: Mount Sunday

The Canterbury Hotel, or 'Brown Pub', Methven, mid-winter

Opposite: Looking down Forest Drive, Methven, to Mt Taylor

Rakaia River and
Canterbury plains
viewed from Mt Hutt

Opposite: Braided
shingle beds of the
upper reaches of the
Rakaia River

Cattle grazing
near Big Ben

Opposite: Cabbage
tree grove on the
upper Rakaia River

Storm clouds gather
over the Rakaia River,
Barrhill

Opposite: Tussock,
Mt Potts

Fence post, Kyle

View of the Pacific coast, Kyle

Hardy plant on a rock face, Rakaia Gorge

Windswept trees by the Harper River

Sheep grazing where the Rakaia and Wilberforce rivers meet near Mt Algidus

Barley crop, Methven

Opposite: Radish seed crop,
Methven

Opposite: Ryton Bay,
Lake Coleridge

Fence, Hakatere-Potts Road

Rakaia River near Blackford, above the gorge

Mt Taylor, behind the Rangitata Diversion Race

Opposite: Mt Hutt in late autumn

Gnarled fence post & barbed wire

Opposite: Carrot seed crop, Methven

Lake Selfe

The Pacific coast, south of the Rakaia River mouth

The Stavely store with
Mt Somers in the
background

Opposite: Moonset at
sunrise, Mt Somers

Lake Camp

Opposite: Bowyers Stream, near Sharplin Falls

Waratah, Zigzag
Road, Rakaia Gorge

Opposite: Lake Camp

Bridge over the
Rakaia Gorge

Opposite: Foreshore,
Lake Coleridge

Road from Mt Algidus

Opposite: Signpost, Algidus Road

A hot air balloon floats by Mt Hutt

Ashburton River in autumn

A bumblebee foraging
in an onion seed crop

Opposite: Onion seed
crop, Pendarves

Road to Erewhon with Mt Sunday on the left and the Cloudy Peak Range in the distance

Frosty strainer post,
Mt Somers

Opposite: Late spring
snowfall, Mt Somers

A lone sheep in the mist, Rakaia Gorge

Sheep among border dykes, Lyndhurst

Gathering nor'west clouds reflected in Lake Heron

Lake Heron

Lake Camp, with the Southern Alps in the distance

Early morning light on Mt Somers

Opposite: The Ashburton River running through the plains

Ripples in the plains captured
from a hot-air balloon

Opposite: Mid-Canterbury plains
and Rakaia River

Ewe and lamb, with Mt Hutt in the background

For copies of this book or prints on canvas of any images within please contact:
Bill Irwin
121 Forest Drive
Methven
Email: bill@fairfieldarts.co.nz
www.billirwin.co.nz

ISBN 0-473-11276-0

Production & design by Hazard Publishing Limited, P.O. Box 2151, Christchurch, New Zealand
Printed in China